AUTISM AND  M

THE NARCISSISTIC EXPERIENCE OF AUTISM, UNDERSTANDING AND MANAGING AUTISM AND NARCISSISM IN RELATIONSHIPS

SARAH ROBERTSSON

CONTENTS

CHAPTER 1

Introduction: Autism and Narcissism

Autism is a neurodevelopmental disorder that affects communication, social interaction, and behavior. Individuals with autism may have difficulty with social cues, understanding and responding appropriately to emotions, and may engage in repetitive behaviors or have strong preferences for routines. They may also experience sensory processing challenges, such as hypersensitivity to noise, light, or touch.

On the other hand, narcissism is a personality disorder characterized by a grandiose sense of self-importance, a lack of empathy, and a need for admiration. Individuals with narcissism may exploit or manipulate others, have a sense of entitlement, and feel superior to others.

The intersection of autism and narcissism in relationships can occur in several ways. For example, individuals with autism may be particularly vulnerable to narcissistic abuse from others, such as being gaslighted or manipulated into believing that their experiences are invalid or wrong. Additionally, individuals with narcissism may struggle to understand and empathize with individuals with autism, leading to conflicts in communication, emotional regulation, and intimacy in relationships.

In short, the intersection of autism and narcissism in relationships can lead to unique challenges for individuals with these conditions, as well as their friends, family members, and mental health professionals who support them. Understanding how these conditions can intersect is an important first step in effectively managing them in relationships.

CHAPTER 2

Understanding Autism

Autism, also known as Autism Spectrum Disorder (ASD), is a neurodevelopmental disorder that affects communication, social interaction, and behavior. It is a spectrum disorder, which means that individuals with autism can present with a wide range of symptoms and severity levels.

One of the defining characteristics of autism is difficulty with social communication and interaction. Individuals with autism may struggle to understand and respond to social cues, such as facial expressions, body language, and tone of voice. They may also have difficulty initiating or maintaining conversations, or may engage in repetitive or rigid behaviors that can make social interaction challenging.

In addition to social difficulties, individuals with autism may also experience sensory processing challenges. They may be hypersensitive to sounds, lights, textures, or other sensory stimuli, which can cause discomfort or anxiety. They may also engage in repetitive behaviors, such as flapping their hands or rocking their bodies, as a way of regulating sensory input.

Another characteristic of autism is a tendency to engage in repetitive or rigid behaviors or routines. For example, an individual with autism may insist on following the same routine every day, or may become upset if their environment or routine is disrupted. They may also have highly specific interests or fascinations, and may be highly knowledgeable about certain topics.

Autism can affect individuals in their daily lives in many ways. It can impact their ability to communicate effectively with others, to understand social cues and social norms, and to form and maintain relationships. It can also impact their ability to regulate their emotions and manage sensory input, which can make everyday activities challenging.

Individuals with autism may face stigma and discrimination, which can impact their access to education, employment, and other opportunities. However, with appropriate support and interventions, individuals with autism can lead fulfilling lives and make meaningful contributions to society.

Types of autism

There are several different types of autism, all of which are characterized by challenges with social interaction, communication, and behavior. Here are some of the different types of autism and their defining characteristics:

1. **Classic autism:** This is the most severe form of autism, characterized by significant challenges with communication, social interaction, and behavior. Individuals with classic autism may have delayed language development or may not speak at all. They may engage in repetitive or self-

injurious behaviors and may have limited interests.

2. **Asperger's Syndrome:** This is a milder form of autism, characterized by challenges with social interaction and communication, but without the significant language delays or intellectual impairments associated with classic autism. Individuals with Asperger's Syndrome may have average or above-average intelligence and may have highly specific interests or fascinations.

3. **Pervasive Developmental Disorder-Not Otherwise Specified (PDD-NOS):** This is a catch-all diagnosis for individuals who have some characteristics of autism, but do not meet the criteria for classic autism or Asperger's Syndrome.

Challenges with social interaction, communication, and sensory processing are common across all types of autism. Here are some of the specific challenges that individuals with autism may face:

1. **Social interaction:** Individuals with autism may struggle to understand social cues and may have difficulty initiating or maintaining conversations. They may also struggle to make eye contact or may engage in repetitive or rigid behaviors that can make social interaction challenging.

2. **Communication:** Many individuals with autism have challenges with communication, ranging from delayed language development to difficulty understanding the nuances of language. They may struggle with figurative language or sarcasm, and may have difficulty understanding the perspectives of others.

3. **Sensory processing:** Individuals with autism may be hypersensitive to sensory stimuli, such as loud noises, bright lights, or certain textures. They may

also engage in repetitive behaviors as a way of regulating sensory input.

CHAPTER 3

Understanding Narcissism

Narcissism is a personality trait that is characterized by an inflated sense of self-importance, a constant need for admiration, and a lack of empathy for others. Individuals who display narcissistic traits may have an excessive sense of entitlement and may engage in grandiose thinking, believing that they are superior to others.

One of the defining characteristics of narcissism is a lack of empathy for others. Individuals with narcissistic traits may struggle to understand the perspectives of others and may not be able to relate to others' emotions. They may also be highly critical of others and may have a tendency to belittle or dismiss the opinions of others.

Individuals with narcissistic traits may also have a need for constant admiration and validation. They may seek out attention and praise from others and may become angry or defensive if they do not receive the attention they believe they deserve. They may also have a sense of entitlement, believing that they deserve special treatment or privileges because of their perceived superiority.

In their daily lives, individuals with narcissistic traits may struggle to form and maintain close relationships. Their lack of empathy and excessive need for attention can make it difficult for them to connect with others on a deeper level. They may also struggle with criticism or rejection, as they may perceive these as personal attacks on their sense of self-worth.

Individuals with narcissistic traits may engage in risky or impulsive behaviors, as they may believe that they are invincible or above the rules that apply to others. This can lead to problems in their personal and professional lives, as they may engage in behaviors that are harmful to themselves or others.

It is important to note that not all individuals who display narcissistic traits have Narcissistic Personality Disorder (NPD), which is a diagnosable mental health condition. However, individuals who do have NPD may experience significant distress and impairment in their daily lives as a result of their symptoms.

Types of narcissism

There are different types of narcissism, but the two most common types are grandiose narcissism and vulnerable narcissism.

1. **Grandiose narcissism:** This type of narcissism is characterized by an inflated sense of self-importance, a need for admiration, and a lack of empathy for others. Individuals with grandiose narcissism may engage in behaviors that reflect their sense of superiority, such as bragging about their accomplishments or belittling others. They may also have a sense of entitlement, believing that they deserve special treatment or privileges.

2. **Vulnerable narcissism:** This type of narcissism is characterized by a more fragile sense of self-esteem and a need for constant validation and reassurance. Individuals with vulnerable narcissism may be more self-critical than those with grandiose narcissism and may be more prone to feelings of anxiety or depression. However, they still struggle with empathy and may have difficulty understanding the perspectives of others.

Both types of narcissism can lead to challenges in relationships. People with narcissistic traits may struggle with empathy, which can make it difficult for them to connect with others on an emotional level. They may also struggle with self-reflection, as they may have a distorted view of themselves and their behaviors.

People with narcissistic traits may have difficulty maintaining healthy relationships, as they may prioritize their own needs and desires over those of their partner.

They may also struggle with criticism or rejection, as these experiences can challenge their sense of self-worth.

Another challenge for people with narcissistic traits is the impact of their behavior on others. Narcissistic behaviors, such as belittling or dismissing the opinions of others, can be hurtful and damaging to those around them. This can lead to strained or broken relationships, both in personal and professional settings.

It is important to note that while individuals with narcissistic traits may face challenges in their relationships, they are not necessarily doomed to have unhealthy relationships. With appropriate support and interventions, individuals with narcissistic traits can learn to manage their behaviors and develop healthier relationships. This may include therapy or counseling to address underlying psychological issues, as well as learning skills to improve empathy and communication.

CHAPTER 4

The Intersection of Autism and Narcissism

The intersection of autism and narcissism in relationships can be complex and challenging. Individuals with autism may struggle with social communication and may have difficulty understanding the perspectives and emotions of others. Meanwhile, individuals with narcissistic traits may have a lack of empathy and may prioritize their own needs and desires over those of their partner. These differences can lead to difficulties in understanding and relating to each other, which can strain the relationship.

One potential area of intersection is in the way that individuals with autism may struggle with self-awareness and self-reflection. This can make it difficult for them to recognize the impact of their behavior on others, and they may unintentionally hurt their partner's feelings without realizing it. Meanwhile, individuals with narcissistic traits may struggle to recognize their own faults and may be resistant to feedback or criticism from their partner. This can create a cycle of misunderstanding and hurt feelings in the relationship.

Another potential area of intersection is in the way that individuals with autism may struggle with social communication. They may have difficulty understanding nonverbal cues or may struggle with initiating and maintaining conversations. Meanwhile, individuals with narcissistic traits may be highly critical of their partner's communication skills and may become impatient or dismissive if their partner struggles to communicate effectively. This can lead to feelings of frustration and rejection on both sides.

Individuals with autism and narcissistic traits may struggle with emotional regulation. Individuals with autism may have difficulty managing their emotions and may become overwhelmed or overstimulated in social situations. Meanwhile, individuals with narcissistic traits may struggle with regulating their emotions in response to perceived criticism or rejection from their partner. This can lead to conflicts and misunderstandings in the relationship.

Individuals with autism can be vulnerable to narcissistic abuse due to their social communication challenges and difficulty understanding social cues and boundaries. They may have a strong desire for social connection but struggle to recognize when someone is taking advantage of them or manipulating them. This can make them susceptible to the manipulative tactics of individuals with narcissistic traits.

Narcissistic individuals often have a need for control and power over others, which can be particularly damaging for individuals with autism who may struggle to assert themselves or advocate for their needs. Narcissistic individuals may use tactics such as gaslighting, manipulation, and emotional abuse to gain control over their partner with autism, who may struggle to recognize these tactics or understand that they are being mistreated.

Individuals with narcissistic traits may struggle to understand and empathize with people with autism due to their lack of empathy and self-absorption. They may become frustrated with their partner's social communication challenges and may not understand why they struggle to understand nonverbal cues or express themselves effectively. This lack of understanding can lead to feelings of invalidation and neglect for individuals with autism, who may feel like their partner doesn't understand or care about their struggles.

In relationships where one partner has autism and the other has narcissistic traits, there can be a power imbalance that can lead to further difficulties. The narcissistic partner may dominate the relationship, leaving the partner with autism feeling marginalized and unheard. This can lead to feelings of isolation and depression for the partner with autism, who may feel like they have no control over the relationship or their own lives.

The characteristics of autism can make individuals with autism vulnerable to narcissistic abuse, while the characteristics of narcissism can make it difficult for individuals with narcissistic traits to understand and empathize with people with autism. It is important for individuals with autism and their loved ones to be aware of these dynamics and seek appropriate support and interventions to promote healthy and respectful relationships.

CHAPTER 5

The Narcissistic Experience of Autism

From the perspective of someone with narcissism, the experience of having autism may be challenging and frustrating. Narcissistic individuals tend to have a grandiose sense of self and a need for admiration and attention from others. They may struggle to understand the social communication challenges and sensory processing differences that individuals with autism experience, and may view these challenges as weaknesses or flaws.

Narcissistic individuals may become frustrated with their partner with autism's difficulty expressing emotions or understanding social cues, and may feel that their partner is not meeting their needs for attention or validation. This can lead to feelings of impatience, irritation, and resentment towards their partner with autism.

Individuals with narcissism may struggle to empathize with their partner's struggles and may have difficulty accepting their partner's differences. They may view their partner with autism as inferior or lacking in social skills, which can further exacerbate the power imbalance in the relationship.

However, it is important to note that not all individuals with narcissism will have negative attitudes towards individuals with autism. Some may recognize and appreciate their partner's unique perspectives and strengths, and may work to support and understand their partner's experiences.

The experience of having autism from the perspective of someone with narcissism can be challenging, as their grandiose sense of self and need for attention may conflict with the social communication challenges and sensory processing differences that individuals with autism experience. It is important for individuals with narcissism to work to develop empathy and understanding towards their partner with autism, and to seek support and interventions to promote healthy and respectful relationships.

Narcissism can impact the way individuals with autism perceive themselves and their experiences in a number of ways.

Firstly, if an individual with autism is in a relationship with someone with narcissistic traits, they may internalize the negative messages and invalidation from their partner. This can lead to feelings of self-doubt, low self-esteem, and a negative self-image. The individual with autism may feel that their partner's negative views of them are accurate, and may struggle to recognize and value their own unique strengths and abilities.

Narcissistic individuals may attempt to control and manipulate their partner with autism, which can further impact the individual's sense of self. The individual with autism may feel that they have to constantly adapt to their partner's expectations, and may lose touch with their own sense of identity and autonomy.

Narcissism can also impact the relationships that individuals with autism have with others. Individuals with autism may struggle with social communication challenges, and may rely on close relationships with others to provide support and validation. If their partner has narcissistic traits, they may struggle to receive the support and validation they need, which can lead to feelings of isolation and loneliness.

If an individual with autism internalizes negative messages and invalidation from their partner, they may struggle to form healthy relationships with others outside of the relationship. They may struggle to recognize their own worth and value, and may have difficulty trusting others.

CHAPTER 6

Understanding and Managing Autism and Narcissism in Relationships

For individuals with autism and narcissism who are in relationships, it can be challenging to navigate the complexities of social communication, empathy, and emotional regulation. However, there are several practical strategies that can help promote healthy and respectful relationships:

1. **Seek support:** Both individuals with autism and narcissism may benefit from seeking support from a therapist, counselor, or support group. Therapy can help individuals with autism develop social communication skills and strategies for managing sensory processing differences, while individuals with narcissism can benefit from interventions aimed at developing empathy and emotional regulation.

2. **Practice active listening:** Active listening involves giving your full attention to the other person, acknowledging their feelings, and reflecting back what they have said. This can help promote empathy and understanding in the relationship.

3. **Practice self-reflection:** Individuals with narcissism may struggle with self-reflection, but it is an important skill for promoting healthy relationships. Taking time to reflect on your thoughts, feelings, and behaviors can help you identify areas for growth and improvement.

4. **Set boundaries:** Boundaries are important in any relationship, and can help promote respect and autonomy. Individuals with autism and narcissism may benefit from setting clear boundaries with their partner, and communicating these boundaries in a clear and respectful manner.

5. **Celebrate differences:** Both individuals with autism and narcissism have unique strengths and challenges. Celebrating these differences can help promote a positive and accepting relationship.

6. **Practice self-care:** Self-care is important for promoting emotional and mental well-being. Individuals with autism and narcissism may benefit from engaging in activities that promote relaxation, such as meditation, yoga, or exercise.

Strategies for improving communication and empathy, managing sensory issues, and setting boundaries.

Improving communication and empathy, managing sensory issues, and setting boundaries are all important skills for individuals with autism and narcissism who are in relationships. Here are some strategies that can help:

1. **Improving communication:** Communication is a key component of any healthy relationship. Individuals with autism may struggle with social

communication, while individuals with narcissism may struggle with active listening and empathy. Some strategies for improving communication include:

- **Practicing active listening:** This involves giving your full attention to the other person, acknowledging their feelings, and reflecting back what they have said. This can help promote empathy and understanding in the relationship.

- **Using clear language:** Individuals with autism may struggle with understanding idiomatic language or sarcasm. Using clear, direct language can help improve communication.

- **Developing social communication skills:** Individuals with autism may benefit from social communication interventions, such as social stories or role-playing exercises.

- **Developing empathy:** Individuals with narcissism may benefit from interventions aimed at developing empathy, such as mindfulness practices or cognitive-behavioral therapy.

2. **Managing sensory issues:** Individuals with autism may be hypersensitive or hyposensitive to sensory stimuli, which can impact their daily lives and relationships. Some strategies for managing sensory issues include:

- **Identifying triggers:** Identifying what triggers sensory overload or discomfort can help individuals with autism manage their sensory issues more effectively.

- **Using sensory tools:** Sensory tools such as fidget toys or noise-cancelling headphones can help individuals with autism manage sensory input.

- **Creating a sensory-friendly environment:** Adjusting the lighting, noise level, or other sensory inputs in the environment can help individuals with autism feel more comfortable and reduce sensory overload.

3. **Setting boundaries:** Boundaries are important in any relationship and can help promote respect and autonomy. Some strategies for setting boundaries include:

- **Identifying your needs:** Knowing what you need from the relationship and what you are comfortable with can help you set appropriate boundaries.

- **Communicating clearly:** Communicating your boundaries in a clear and respectful manner can help promote understanding and respect in the relationship.

- **Enforcing boundaries:** Following through with consequences when boundaries are crossed can help reinforce their importance and promote respect in the relationship.

Challenges of navigating a relationship where one person has autism and the other has narcissism

Navigating a relationship where one person has autism and the other has narcissism can be challenging. Both autism and narcissism can impact how individuals perceive and interact with the world, which can make it difficult for them to understand each other's perspectives and needs. Here are some specific challenges that may arise in such a relationship:

1. **Communication difficulties:** Individuals with autism may struggle with social communication, while individuals with narcissism may struggle with active listening and empathy. This can lead to misunderstandings, frustration, and a lack of emotional connection in the relationship.

2. **Different social and emotional needs:** Individuals with autism may have different social and emotional needs than individuals with narcissism. For example, individuals with autism may prefer more structured and predictable social interactions, while individuals with narcissism may crave attention and validation from others.

3. **Sensory issues:** Individuals with autism may be hypersensitive or hyposensitive to sensory stimuli, while individuals with narcissism may be more focused on their own needs and desires. This can make it difficult to create a comfortable and sensory-friendly environment for both individuals.

4. **Boundary issues:** Individuals with autism may struggle with setting and enforcing boundaries, while individuals with narcissism may have difficulty respecting others' boundaries. This can lead to issues with personal space, autonomy, and emotional safety in the relationship.

5. **Lack of empathy and understanding:** Individuals with autism and narcissism may struggle to understand and empathize with each other's experiences and perspectives. This can lead to a lack of emotional connection and difficulty in building trust and intimacy in the relationship.

CHAPTER 7

Supporting Individuals with Autism and Narcissism

Friends, family members, and mental health professionals can play an important role in supporting individuals with autism and narcissism. Here are some ways they can provide support:

1. **Education and understanding:** Friends, family members, and mental health professionals can learn about autism and narcissism to better understand the experiences of individuals with these conditions. This can include learning about the specific challenges and strengths associated with each condition, as well as effective communication strategies and coping techniques.

2. **Validation and empathy:** Individuals with autism and narcissism may feel misunderstood or

marginalized due to the stigma and misconceptions surrounding their conditions. Friends, family members, and mental health professionals can provide validation and empathy by acknowledging their experiences and feelings, and showing support and acceptance.

3. **Encouragement and motivation:** Individuals with autism and narcissism may struggle with self-esteem and motivation. Friends, family members, and mental health professionals can provide encouragement and motivation by celebrating their achievements, helping them set realistic goals, and providing positive feedback.

4. **Practical support:** Friends, family members, and mental health professionals can provide practical support by helping individuals with autism and narcissism with everyday tasks, such as organizing schedules, managing finances, and finding employment.

5. **Referral to resources:** Friends, family members, and mental health professionals can refer individuals with autism and narcissism to resources such as support groups, therapy, and community programs that can provide additional support and resources.

It is important to note that each individual with autism and narcissism is unique, and may require different types and levels of support. The best way to provide support is to listen to their needs, offer non-judgmental support and guidance, and collaborate with them to develop a plan that works for their individual needs and circumstances.

When supporting individuals with autism and narcissism, it is important to focus on building understanding and empathy, providing practical support, and seeking professional help when necessary. Here are some strategies for each:

1. **Building understanding and empathy:**

- Learn about the specific challenges and strengths associated with autism and narcissism, and how they can intersect in relationships.

- Take time to listen to the individual and their experiences, and try to understand their perspective.

- Avoid judgment and assumptions, and approach the individual with empathy and acceptance.

2. **Providing practical support:**

- Offer to help with everyday tasks, such as organizing schedules, managing finances, and finding employment.

- Provide opportunities for socialization and support, such as connecting the individual with groups or activities that align with their interests.

- Help the individual develop coping strategies and problem-solving skills, and offer practical solutions to challenges they may face.

3. **Seeking professional help when necessary:**

- Encourage the individual to seek professional help, such as therapy or counseling, if they are struggling with their mental health or relationships.

- Offer to help them find a qualified mental health professional who has experience working with individuals with autism and/or narcissism.

- Support the individual in adhering to their treatment plan, and offer to attend therapy or counseling sessions with them if they are comfortable with it.

CHAPTER 8

The Role of Therapy in Managing Autism and Narcissism in Relationships

Therapy can play an important role in managing autism and narcissism in relationships. Here are some ways in which therapy can be helpful:

1. **Improving communication skills:** Many individuals with autism and/or narcissism struggle with communication and social skills, which can make it difficult to form and maintain relationships. Therapy can help these individuals develop more effective communication skills, such as active listening, assertiveness, and conflict resolution.

2. **Developing empathy and understanding:** Individuals with autism and/or narcissism may struggle with empathy and understanding of others' perspectives. Therapy can help individuals

with autism and/or narcissism develop more empathy and understanding of others' experiences, which can improve their ability to form and maintain relationships.

3. **Managing sensory issues:** Many individuals with autism and/or narcissism have sensory processing issues that can make certain environments or situations overwhelming. Therapy can provide strategies for managing sensory issues and developing coping mechanisms for sensory overload.

4. **Setting boundaries:** Individuals with autism and/or narcissism may struggle with setting and maintaining healthy boundaries in relationships. Therapy can help individuals learn how to set appropriate boundaries and communicate their needs effectively.

5. **Managing co-occurring mental health conditions:** Many individuals with autism and/or narcissism may also have co-occurring mental health conditions, such as anxiety or depression. Therapy can help individuals manage these conditions and develop effective coping strategies.

Types of therapy that may be helpful for individuals with autism and narcissism

There are several types of therapy that may be helpful for individuals with autism and narcissism in managing their conditions in relationships. Here are some examples:

1. **Cognitive-behavioral therapy (CBT):** CBT is a type of therapy that focuses on changing negative patterns of thinking and behavior. It can be helpful for individuals with autism and/or narcissism who struggle with communication, social skills, and emotional regulation.

2. **Acceptance and commitment therapy (ACT):** ACT is a type of therapy that emphasizes mindfulness and acceptance of one's thoughts and feelings. It can be helpful for individuals with autism and/or narcissism who struggle with anxiety, depression, or emotional regulation.

3. **Social skills training:** Social skills training is a type of therapy that focuses on developing communication and social skills. It can be helpful for individuals with autism and/or narcissism who struggle with forming and maintaining relationships.

4. **Sensory integration therapy:** Sensory integration therapy is a type of therapy that focuses on managing sensory processing issues. It can be helpful for individuals with autism and/or narcissism who struggle with sensory overload or sensory seeking behaviors.

Finding the right therapist for individuals with autism and narcissism can be challenging. Here are some strategies that may be helpful:

1. Look for a therapist with experience working with individuals with autism and/or narcissism. It is important to find a therapist who understands the unique challenges that these conditions can present in relationships.

2. Consider the therapeutic approach. Different therapeutic approaches may be more or less effective for individuals with autism and/or narcissism. Research different approaches and discuss with the therapist which approach may be most effective.

3. Seek recommendations from trusted sources. Ask friends, family members, or mental health professionals for recommendations on therapists who may be a good fit.

Working effectively with a therapist requires open communication and collaboration. Here are some strategies that may be helpful:

1. Be honest and open about your experiences and concerns. It is important to communicate openly with the therapist in order to get the most out of therapy.

2. Set clear goals for therapy. Discuss with the therapist what you hope to achieve through therapy and work together to develop a plan to achieve those goals.

3. Be patient and persistent. Therapy can be a long and challenging process, but with persistence and patience, it can be a valuable tool for managing autism and narcissism in relationships.

CHAPTER 9

Looking to the Future

As research into autism and narcissism continues to evolve, there is potential for new treatments and therapies to emerge that can better address the unique challenges faced by individuals with these conditions in relationships. For example, researchers may explore the potential of therapies that focus on improving communication and social skills, such as cognitive-behavioral therapy and social skills training.

There may also be a growing recognition of the importance of addressing both autism and narcissism in therapy, rather than viewing them as separate issues. This could involve developing new therapeutic approaches that take into account the ways in which these two conditions can intersect and impact individuals in relationships.

As technology continues to advance, there may be new opportunities to develop interventions that can support individuals with autism and narcissism in their daily lives. For example, virtual reality technology could be used to create immersive environments that help individuals with autism practice social skills, while online therapy platforms could make it easier for individuals with narcissism to access support.

The future of research into autism and narcissism is promising, and there is potential for new treatments and therapies that can improve the lives of individuals with these conditions and their relationships with others.

Importance of raising awareness of the intersection of autism and narcissism

Raising awareness of the intersection of autism and narcissism is crucial for creating a more inclusive and understanding society. It is important to recognize that individuals with these conditions may face unique challenges in relationships, and that there are strategies and resources available to support them.

By increasing awareness of the ways in which autism and narcissism can intersect, we can help to reduce stigma and promote acceptance and understanding. This can involve education and outreach efforts aimed at the general public, as well as targeted initiatives aimed at healthcare providers, educators, and other professionals who work with individuals with these conditions.

Creating a more inclusive and understanding society also requires a commitment to empathy and compassion. This means recognizing that everyone has unique strengths and challenges, and that we all have something to contribute to our communities.

It also means advocating for policies and practices that support individuals with autism and narcissism. This could include promoting workplace accommodations for individuals with these conditions, ensuring access to quality healthcare and mental health services, and providing funding for research into new treatments and therapies.

Creating a more inclusive and understanding society requires a willingness to listen and learn from individuals with autism and narcissism themselves, as well as their families and caregivers. By working together to promote awareness, understanding, and acceptance, we can build a more supportive and compassionate world for all.

CHAPTER 10

Conclusion

This book, "Autism and Narcissism: The Narcissistic Experience of Autism, Understanding and Managing Autism and Narcissism in Relationships," explores the intersection of autism and narcissism in relationships, providing insights and strategies for individuals with these conditions, as well as their loved ones and mental health professionals.

Importance of empathy and understanding in relationships

Empathy and understanding are crucial components of building strong and healthy relationships between individuals with autism and narcissism. While these conditions may present challenges to communication and connection, it is possible to overcome these barriers with the right strategies and approaches.

One key strategy for building empathy and understanding is active listening. This involves truly listening to the other person, focusing on their words and emotions, and reflecting back what you hear to ensure understanding. This can be particularly helpful for individuals with autism, who may struggle with interpreting social cues and nonverbal communication.

Another important strategy is to practice self-awareness and self-reflection. This is particularly important for individuals with narcissism, who may struggle with empathy and self-awareness. By taking the time to reflect on their own thoughts and feelings, individuals with narcissism can better understand the perspectives and experiences of others.

It is also important to practice patience and compassion in relationships involving autism and narcissism. These conditions may make communication and connection more challenging, but with patience and understanding, it is possible to build stronger and more fulfilling relationships.

Printed in Great Britain
by Amazon

43291412R00036